Creation Inspirations

A New View of the World Around You

Cheryl Pickett

Be Inspired!
Cheryl Pickett

Copyright © 2009, 2013

Published by:
Brighter Day Publishing
USA

Contact/Orders:
www.creationinspirations.com
www.cherylpickett.com

Printed in the United States of America
ISBN: 978-0-9841855-0-4

Cover & Interior Design: Carolyn Sheltraw

Table of Contents

Aardvark

What Do They Look Like?

Is it a pig? An anteater? Is it related to rabbits or kangaroos? Even though aardvarks do look like several of these animals, in reality, they aren't related to any of them at all.

Aardvarks are literally one of a kind; there aren't any other animals like them. Their long, tube-like nose, pointy ears, thick, tapered tail and unique teeth even put them in their own scientific category.

Where Do They Live?

There's an easy way to remember where aardvarks live in the wild; their name starts with "a" and so does the name of the continent where they live-Africa.

Specifically, they live in sub-Saharan Africa, which means they live in areas south of the Sahara Desert. They can be found on the plains and grasslands, as well as in forests. They move around to wherever they can find the most food.

What Do They Eat?

The answer to this question is also easy to remember because there are only two things on a wild aardvark's menu – ants and termites.

Aardvarks are nocturnal and go out each night in search of new termite mounds or ant nests. They use their nose to sniff them out as well as their ears. Their hearing is so sensitive they can even hear insect activity underground!

Once they find a good spot, they use their strong claws to pull apart hard, dry termite mounds or to dig up anthills. Thick, tough skin keeps them from being bitten or stung. They use their long, super sticky tongues to pull the insects into their mouth and they consume thousands of them every single day.

More Interesting Stuff

Aardvarks generally move slowly when they walk, but when it comes to digging, they can be lightning fast. If an aardvark senses danger or is under attack by a predator, it can dig a hole in a matter of seconds and close it up behind itself, keeping the enemy out. Once it believes the danger has passed, it will peek out, make sure the coast is clear, and then return to life as usual.

A New View

Many animals eat fruit, grass or leaves, but some eat other creatures, and that makes mealtime a bit more challenging. Aardvarks fall into the second group; they eat termites and ants, which as you can guess, would prefer not to be lunch.

As an aardvark claws into a termite mound, hundreds of the tiny creatures swarm around it, biting and stinging to annoy the aardvark and, hopefully, make it go away. Luckily, for aardvarks, (not so much for the termites) God gave them thick skin and a tough tongue to protect it and enable it to keep eating instead of being scared off.

Mealtime for aardvarks reminds us of our lives as Christians. No matter who we are, or where we live, there will be times when people around us will try to annoy us and get us to stop believing or witnessing for Christ. They use words that sting our hearts; sometimes they may try to hurt our bodies too. However, God knows this and promises that He will give us what we need to keep going.

The next time you see an aardvark:
Think about what it's like for them to eat termites and how God created them with what they need to do it. Remember that God gives us what we need to keep going when people try to annoy us or attack us because of our faith in Him.

Bible Verses

Psalm 55:12

If an enemy were
insulting me, I could
endure it; if a foe
were raising himself
against me, I could
hide from him.

1 Thessalonians 2:2

We had previously suffered
and been insulted in
Philippi, as you know, but
with the help of our God we
dared to tell you his gospel
in spite of strong opposition.

A Sticky Situation

To Do & Discover

Aardvarks get the food they want by using their speedy, sticky tongues to grab it. While it's too messy to pick up your food with your tongue, there are other ways experience a little of what it's like to be an aardvark. Are you ready for A Sticky Situation?

What You Need:

An unsharpened pencil, a retractable pen or even a stick will do

2 kinds of tape such as scotch tape and duct tape or masking tape (if you only have one kind it's okay)

A couple dozen paper clips and various other small or lightweight items

Extra Fact:

Aardvarks can shut their nostrils completely so that dust or termites can't get in.

What to Do:

1. Wrap the tip of your pencil, pen or stick with scotch tape with the "sticky" facing outward. To do this, start wrapping normally with the "sticky" touching the pencil going about halfway around to secure it on, then go the other way and start wrapping so the "sticky" faces out. You only need to go around three or four times.

2. Now it's time to use your "aardvark tongue". Try picking up different size pieces of paper. Don't push them on too hard because you need to be able to get them off. Once you have the hang of it, see what else you can pick up. See how heavy an item has to be before you can't hold on.

3. Try this activity again, but use a different kind of tape. Can you pick up bigger objects now?

4. Now it's time to find out how speedy you are. Spread out ten to twelve paperclips on a table or counter top in front of you. These are your "termites." Make sure there's a little space in between each one, but don't spread them too far. Put a small bowl or cup next to you.

5. Have someone else time you with a stopwatch or clock. When time starts, grab one paperclip at a time with your "aardvark tongue", take it off and put it into the bowl. See how fast you can collect them all. If it's too easy, try spreading out the paperclips a bit more. Challenge your friends or family to see who's the fastest termite picker upper!

American Alligator

What Do They Look Like?

Have you ever wondered about how to tell the difference between an alligator and a crocodile? It really isn't that hard once you know what to look for.

The first thing to look at is the nose, also called a snout. If you're looking at an alligator, you'll see a wide, rounded snout. If it's a crocodile, it will look like a long triangle that tapers to a narrow point.

Next, look at the mouth and teeth. Alligators are able to close their mouths with all of their teeth inside. If you can see a tooth sticking out along the lower jaw near the back, it's a crocodile.

Where Do They Live?

As their name suggests, American alligators are found in America, specifically North America. They live in freshwater swamps, marshes and lakes because they cannot tolerate saltwater for very long. In the wild, they can be found in the southeastern states from Texas to North Carolina. The state most well known for being home to gators is Florida. In fact, the alligator is their official state reptile.

What Do They Eat?

Alligators are definitely carnivorous, meaning they only eat meat. They'll try to catch almost any kind of animal that walks, crawls or swims near enough when it's time to eat. When they're small, they eat little things like worms. Once they're adults they may capture prey as large as deer and cows. Like the big cats of Africa, alligators play a very important role at the top of the food chain.

More Interesting Stuff

Alligators reproduce by laying eggs. Females build a nest out of twigs, leaves and mud and then lay dozens of eggs at a time. She covers them with more plants and dirt. The eggs stay warm because heat is created as the nest materials naturally start to decay.

One very unique characteristic about alligator eggs is that temperature decides whether each hatchling will be a male or female. Embryos that get the warmest are born male; the cooler ones will be female. If the temperature is sort of medium warm all over the nest, about half will be male and half female.

When the babies are ready to be born, they make a squeaky noise as loud as they can to tell the mother it's time to uncover them. The babies also have a sharp tip at the end of their nose so they can crack their eggshell from the inside. After the babies hatch, the mothers stay around and protect their young for several months.

A New View

When you think of an alligator, what comes to mind? Do you think of a cuddly animal that you could snuggle up to? Probably not, unless one of your favorite stuffed animals happens to be an alligator.

Most people think of alligators as tough and dangerous. This makes sense because they aren't soft or snuggly at all. Their skin is thick and covered with bony plates and scales that protect them similar to the armor that knights or soldiers wear. Alligators also have powerful jaws and the most forceful bite of any animal on earth. All of these traits help them to survive and defend themselves.

As Christians, God gives us our own armor and strength through the words of the Bible so that we can defend our faith when we need to.

The next time you see an American Alligator:
Remember what powerful creatures they are and that you too can be strong and powerful through faith in God. No matter what happens in your life, God promises that His love and strength is there to help you.

Bible Verse

Ephesians 6: 10-11

Finally, be strong in the Lord and in his mighty power.
Put on the full armor of God so that you
can take your stand against the devil's schemes.

Grinnin' Gator

To Do & Discover

Sometimes drawing animals is a bit of a challenge. Here's an easy way to draw an alligator anytime you want with a special template that's always "at hand."

What You Need:

White or green construction paper

Green paint, markers or crayons

Pencil

What to Do:

1. Put the paper on your work surface horizontally (long side on top).

2. Put your left hand flat on the paper near the right edge with your fingers pointing toward the right. Put your fingers together; point your thumb down making a V shape between thumb and first finger.

3. Trace around your hand with the pencil. This is your alligator's head.

4. Add a body, legs, eyes, and teeth to finish your alligator.

5. If you used white paper, paint or color your alligator green. If you used green paper, you can cut it out if you want.

6. If you have room on the page, draw in the swamp or lake where your alligator lives.

Extra Fact:

Alligators swallow their food whole or large pieces. Teeth are mainly used for gripping, not chewing.

Arctic Fox

What Do They Look Like?

Compared to other fox species, arctic foxes are heavier, somewhat chunky, have shorter legs and extra thick fur. All of these traits help them conserve body heat so they can survive the arctic cold.

Another special characteristic of arctic foxes is that they change color twice a year! If the fox lives in the far northern parts of their territory, their coat is white in the winter and brown gray in the summer. In other areas, they are bluish gray in the winter and darker brown in the summer. These color changes camouflage the arctic fox against its surrounding so that it can hunt efficiently.

14

Where Do They Live?

Arctic foxes live as close to the top of the world as you can get. They are found in the Arctic regions of several areas including America, Canada and Scandinavia.

Also, unlike many animals that live in a small territory, arctic foxes are nomadic, which means they don't stay in one place very long. They travel many miles during the year as they hunt for food.

What Do They Eat?

When it comes to food, arctic foxes will eat almost anything. They are omnivores which means they'll eat plants or animals depending on what's available.

During the summer, they like to eat mostly small mammals like moles and lemmings. At other times during the year, they'll also eat bird eggs, fish and some plants. Occasionally, when they can't find enough food on their own, they'll even finish scraps left by other animals.

More Interesting Stuff

Life on the Arctic tundra is not just cold; it's often twenty, thirty or more degrees below zero during the winter. This means that anything that lives there has to be specially equipped to survive in very harsh conditions. Amazingly, arctic foxes are active year round and do not wait out the cold by hibernating.

One survival skill arctic foxes have is the ability to find their prey even when they can't see it. They can actually hear lemmings in underground burrows that are totally covered by snow. They also have an excellent sense of smell that allows them to find small white birds called ptarmigans which are hard to see on the bright, white snow.

A New View

After traveling and hunting for food by themselves for part of the year, each spring arctic foxes come back together at a den where new pups will be born and raised.

Usually, there is a male and female pair along with other related females who help raise the new babies. Many families return to the same den year after year.

When the babies are strong enough, everyone leaves the den and starts traveling again. They'll do this their whole lives. When the pups are adults, they'll continue the cycle they learned from their parents, and many will return to the same dens with their pups that they went to with their parents.

Our Christian life is a lot like this. Our families take us to God's house when we're young where we learn, grow, and return again and again. Then when we're adults, it is our turn to raise children to know the love of God and to come to faith in Him. Sometimes we all stay at the same church too.

The next time you see an arctic fox: Remember how they return to their family dens and how wonderful it is to be able to go to church again and again as the family of God.

Bible Verse

Psalm 90: 1

Lord, you have been our
dwelling place throughout
all generations.

Home Sweet Home

To Do & Discover

Dens are a very important part of arctic fox life. When males need to dig a new one, they take great care to make sure it is that it will be warm, dry and that it will keep their family as safe as possible.

What You Need:

Something to build with such as:

Wooden blocks

Lego™ blocks

Couch cushions and pillows

What to Do:

1. Pretend you are part of a fox pack and it is your job to build a new den. First, you want to choose somewhere safe and comfortable.

2. Next, think about what kind of den you want to make. How many rooms will it have? How many family members will fit inside? You could also include a special emergency exit or tunnel (arctic fox dens have those). Add any other special features you'd like.

3. Start building!

4. When you're done, show your family the new den. Let them know they are welcome. If you have relatives nearby, invite them over to see and enjoy it too.

Extra Fact:

Because they live where there's bright sun and glare from the snow, arctic foxes' eyes have special pigments that provide natural protection. It's like never taking off your sunglasses!

Bald Eagle

What Do They Look Like?

The first important fact to know about bald eagles is that they aren't really bald! There are some birds that truly lack feathers on their heads, but the bald eagle isn't one of them. It actually gets its name from another definition of "bald" which means "white." Adults also have bright yellow beaks and talons.

Another interesting fact is that they do not get their white heads for four or five years. Bald eagle chicks start out with fluffy, white downy feathers that mature to the dark brown ones they'll have the rest of their lives. At that time, their heads are brown too.

Where Do They Live?

The United States, Canada and Mexico are the only places where bald eagles can be seen in the wild. The biggest populations are in Alaska and the Pacific Northwest areas of Canada, but many other states and provinces have them as well.

Bald eagles live close to water where there's plenty of food. They prefer to build their nests high in the treetops, often 40-50 feet off the ground.

This is actually quite an amazing feat of architecture because nests are often five feet wide, several feet deep and can weigh hundreds of pounds. Occasionally, wind or weak branches can cause a nest to fall. If that happens, the pair that built it will start again nearby.

What Do They Eat?

 Plants are not on the menu for bald eagles at all; they are true carnivores. They are also in the category of "sea eagles" because most of their diet is fish. They will also eat small birds and mammals too. For the most part, if they can catch and carry it away, they'll eat it.

More Interesting Stuff

At one time, when Europeans first settled in the US, there were hundreds of thousands of bald eagles across the continent. The population began to shrink though as people started fishing in the areas where the eagles lived. After World War II, people also began using strong pesticides that caused problems for the birds and they could not reproduce very well.

By the 1960's there were less than 1,000 birds left in the wild. Luckily, some ecologists and scientists felt it was important to save this majestic bird and they began to work hard to make it happen.

The survival of bald eagles is a wonderful success story for conservationists. Today, there are well over 100,000 birds in the wild and they are no longer on the endangered list because of all those efforts to save them.

A New View

"And we will soar on wings like eagles." Have you ever read these words in the Bible or have you heard them in a song? Do you know what they mean? After all, we can't sprout wings and fly, right?

Bald eagles (and other eagles) are known for their ability to fly high, but also for their ability to glide. They float on air currents called thermals, sort of like a boat or a surfboard floats on waves. Using the lift of those air currents, they can go up and up, sometimes as far as three miles into the sky.

Also, when they float in the air like that, they hardly flap their wings. This means they aren't using much of their own energy; they're relying on the air current to lift them up. It also means they can do this for quite a while without tiring out.

In the Bible, the prophet Isaiah tells us that putting our hope or trust in the Lord is like having eagles' wings. This means that we can let Him lift us up when we're tired and that He gives us the strength to get through whatever we're dealing with in our lives. We are able to do more with His help than we can by ourselves.

The next time you see a bald eagle: Picture it flying high in the sky being carried on the air currents. Remember that God lifts us up and that with His power, we can accomplish many things we cannot do on our own.

Bible Verse

Isaiah 40:30-31

Even youths grow tired and weary, and young men stumble and fall; but those who hope in the LORD will renew their strength. They will soar on wings like eagles; they will run and not grow weary, they will walk and not be faint.

Glide Glide Glide

To Do & Discover

Bald eagles are known for their ability to glide on air currents. They appear to float almost effortlessly above the ground for long periods of time. When people started to build aircraft, they looked to birds like the eagle for inspiration and ideas. Let's explore some of those ideas using paper and a little imagination.

What You Need:

Several sheets of 8½ x 11˝ paper

The internet, the library or books you already have about paper airplanes

Extra Fact:

Bald eagles can swim! They don't do it very often but sometimes they are pulled into the water by a heavy fish. When that happens, they have to let go of the fish then swim to shore to dry their feathers.

What to Do:

1. Either online or in books, find instructions for making paper airplanes. Look specifically for ones called "gliders" or descriptions that talk about "gliding."

2. Choose at least three.

3. Make them following the instructions.

4. Decorate them with crayons or markers if you'd like.

5. Try them out and see which one glides and stays in the air the longest. It may not travel the furthest. Make sure you do this in a safe area where they won't hit anybody or anything.

6. Try again and see if you get the same results. See if you can get the worst glider to improve by adjusting it, but you cannot start over and make a completely new one.

7. Once you are confident you have a super gliding design, challenge your friends and family to see if they can match or beat your plane's best glide time.

Bird of Paradise

What Do They Look Like?

For many animals, the answer to the question "What Do They Look Like?" is very simple. Penguins, for example, are generally black and white, tigers are orange with black stripes. However, coming up with easy answers like that is not the case with birds of paradise (we'll call them BOPs for short).

These eye-catching birds come in color combinations you'd probably never imagine. For example, one species, Lawes Parotia, is black with a bluish purple neck, silver white forehead and greenish gold chest. Not only that, the inside of its mouth is lime green!

In addition, many males have special decorative feathers. These feathers might look like wirey antennas or pom-poms over their foreheads. Several species also have plumes or tail feathers that are longer than their whole body!

As is the case with many bird species, females are not normally as colorful as the males.

Where Do They Live?

In the wild, BOPs live in the southern hemisphere in Papua New Guinea, parts of Indonesia and Australia. Most live in tropical mountain forests, including areas called cloud or moss forests.

Birds of Paradise are not found in very many places but luckily, at this time, they are not in danger of extinction.

What Do They Eat?

BOPs are a lot like other birds when it comes to mealtime; their favorite foods are fruits and berries. Sometime they also eat insects and seeds.

More Interesting Stuff

Besides being known for their cool colors and crazy feathers, believe it or not, BOPs are famous for their dancing! Males create elaborate dance performances to get the attention of the females in their area.

They stand on a tree branch or even clear a spot on the ground where the sunshine is brightest, just like an actor or dancer on stage. They spin, shake, or jump up and down while also showing off those fancy feathers. The best dancers are rewarded with the company of lots of females.

A New View

Think of your favorite place in the whole, wide world. Where do you love to visit over and over as often as you can? Where do you wish you could stay forever and not go home?

Now what if you could make this place even better? What would you do? Even if you don't think it's possible, try to think of one thing you could add or take away to make your visits as close to perfect as possible. Have that pictured in your mind? Great! A lot of people call that kind of wonderful place "paradise".

Now think about this; as wonderful as your favorite place is, even if it's almost perfect, it doesn't even come close to what God's paradise, heaven, will be like someday.

We can only begin to imagine what it will be like to live in God's presence in a perfect place forever. But it's fun to try isn't it?

The next time you see a Bird of Paradise:
Remember God's promise that those who believe in Him will someday live in paradise forever. Try to imagine how beautiful it will be.

Bible Verse

Luke 23:42-43

Then he said, "Jesus, remember me when you come into your kingdom." Jesus answered him, "I tell you the truth, today you will be with me in paradise."

Dance of the Lord

To Do & Discover

Male BOPs are known for the dances they do to attract a mate. God's children dance for lots of reasons, including to praise Him. Here's how to make your own special "feathers" that you can use to dance and glorify your heavenly Father.

What You Need:

1. A piece of dowel rod approximately ¼ to ½ inch in diameter, and 12 to 16 inches long. You can also use a ruler or wrapping paper tube.

2. Three pieces of ribbon, any color, about ½ inch to 1 inch wide. Make sure the ribbon is at least a couple inches longer than your rod.

If you don't have ribbon, you can use pieces of yarn, or strips of a thin, lightweight paper like wrapping or tissue paper, or strips of cloth.

3. Glue or thumbtacks.

What to Do:

1. Attach each piece of ribbon (or whatever material you are using) to the rod with either glue or thumbtacks.

   If you use thumbtacks, you'll want to tap them in with a hammer to make sure they're secure. You can put the ribbons near each other or farther apart down the length of the rod.

2. Pick a favorite piece of praise music and make up a dance routine using your new "feathers". If you have family members or friends that also dance or play musical instruments, invite them to join you too!

3. If you don't want to or are unable to dance, you can still use your "feathers" to praise God while you sing or listen to music even if you're sitting in a chair.

Extra Fact:

BOPs almost went extinct about a hundred years ago because people wanted their feathers to decorate women's hats. This practice was declared illegal in the 1920's.

Brown Bear

What Do They Look Like?

Let's start with a question - what color is a brown bear? Sound like a trick question? It isn't. Brown bears can be any one of several shades of brown all the way from yellowy beige, to reddish brown to almost black.

In North America, people use a few different names for brown bears, but they're still talking about the same species. In Alaska for example, they are called both Alaskan brown bears and Kodiak bears. These names refer to where they live. In the western states of the US and western provinces of Canada, brown bears are known as grizzly bears. The word "grizzled" or "grizzly" means "partly gray" and refers to this group of bears' silver-tipped fur.

It's also important to know that even though brown bears may have nearly black fur, they are not the same species as the American black bear. Three ways to tell them apart are: brown bears have a hump on their back at their shoulders, they have a flat, dish shaped face and they have short ears.

Where Do They Live?

The strongest populations of brown bears are in Russia, Canada and Alaska in the USA. Even though the Yellowstone National Park area is known for grizzlies, the population there is dangerously close to disappearing.

Even though at one time there were many bears there, there are less than a thousand now.

Brown bears live in forests, fields and in the mountains. Once they are grown and leave their mothers, they spend a lot of time alone mainly coming together during mating or to share a food source.

What Do They Eat?

Brown bears will eat almost anything they can find that is edible. They eat plants, berries, grasses and roots, along with small mammals and insects. If they live near the water, they also really like to eat fish. Occasionally, they'll also scare other animals away from their food so they can eat it instead.

More Interesting Stuff

Brown bears are powerful diggers. An important group of muscles that make their arms very strong forms the hump on their back. They also have long, tough claws that are perfect for getting through all kinds of dirt.

Digging skills are important in brown bear life for both food and shelter. They use them to pull up tasty roots and bulbs when they're hungry, and to make their dens each winter when it's time to hibernate.

33

A New View

Did you know that bears know a lot about building a home? Each year, they need a new den when it's time to hibernate. Their claws are very strong so they could dig one just about anywhere they wanted to. But they don't; they search for and build in areas that meet special "bear building codes."

When they look for a den site, they look for a place where the ground is solid instead of crumbly, and where there's a rock or a hollow tree to give extra protection during bad weather. In northern climates, they'll also try to find areas where the ground won't freeze too deep.

Pretty smart, right? If you were going to build a house, you'd probably look for a place to build that had many of those same characteristics.

In the Bible, God tells us that when we listen to and apply His "code" to our lives, it is like choosing a solid place to build a house. If we build our lives on a strong foundation (God's word), we won't fall apart when we are hit by the storms and troubles of life.

The next time you see a brown bear:
Remember what smart builders they are and how we also need to be wise as we build our lives with God's word as our strong foundation

Bible Verse

Matthew 7:24-25

Therefore, everyone who hears these words of mine and puts them into practice is like a wise man who built his house on the rock. The rain came down, the streams rose, and the winds blew and beat against that house; yet it did not fall, because it had its foundation on the rock.

Berry Berry Delicious

To Do & Discover

Even though many photos of brown bears show them catching fish, a lot of the time they eat plants and berries. Of course, berries are great food for people too. Here are just a few of the yummy things you can do with them.

What You Need:

Berries! Blueberries, raspberries, or blackberries (which are the kinds brown bears could find in the wild)

If you're in an area where you can pick fresh berries, either in the wild or at a farm, take time to do it. It's a great way for your family to spend an hour or two together outdoors. If you can't pick them fresh, visit your local grocery store or farmers market. Frozen berries are also okay if you can't find fresh.

How much you'll need will depend on what you choose to do with the berries and how many people will be eating what you make.

Extra Fact:

Female brown bears give birth while they're hibernating! The babies nurse and grow through the winter and are ready to follow mom outside the den when she wakes up.

What to Do:

1. **Mix 'em In**
   Mix about a half to ¾ cup berries into muffin or pancake batter.

   (Most people think of blueberries for this purpose but raspberries are fantastic too.)

2. **Top It**
   Top pancakes, waffles, cereal, yogurt or ice cream with your favorite kind of berries.

   Berries also make pretty cake decorations. Put a few berries on the top of frosted cupcakes or pile some in the center of a round cake just before serving. (Make sure they are well drained & not too juicy.)

3. **Layer 'em**
   Layer berries, cubes of your favorite cake or pudding and whipped topping in parfait glasses. If you don't have dessert glasses, water goblets or a big glass bowl work well, too.

4. **Be a bear**
   Nothing fancy this time- just you, a bowl of berries and your fingers - don't forget the napkins!

Camel

What Do They Look Like?

There are two types of camels. Do you know what the difference is? If you said some have one hump and some have two, you're right! Dromedary camels (also called Arabian camels) have one hump; those with two are Bactrian camels.

An easy way to remember which is which is to think about the first letter in their name when it is capitalized. The capital D in Dromedary has one bump, the capital B in Bactrian has two. The rest of this section will focus on dromedary camels.

Where Do They Live?

Most dromedary camels live in the Middle East and Africa. They still play an important role in several cultures that rely on them for meat, milk, and transportation. There are only a few camels living in the wild and those are mainly in Australia. The majority are domesticated, which means raised by people just like farmers raise cattle and donkeys.

What Do They Eat?

Because they live in the desert, dromedary camels have a basic diet that includes the few grasses and plants that grow there. They'll even eat plants that have thorns. One unique feature camels have is a split upper lip. The separation allows each side of their lip to move independently which helps them grip and eat short grass.

Eating plants that have moisture in them sometimes has to substitute for drinking water.

More Interesting Stuff

Have you ever been on a dusty road or at the beach when it's windy? If you get dust or sand in your eyes it stings, doesn't it? Camels live where there's lots of sand and it's often very windy. Luckily, they have a special membrane they can close over each eye to keep the sand out. It's different from a normal eyelid because they can see through it, kind of like wearing goggles.

Another interesting and amazing fact about camels is that they can travel long periods without food and about a week without water. This is partly because of their hump. The hump stores fat (not water) that they can use for energy if they cannot find enough food. If they've gone several days without water, they will drink gallons and gallons at one time to satisfy their thirst.

A New View

Have you ever tried to walk in a big pile of sand, loose dirt or gravel? Or how about across a beach or sand dune? It's not as easy as walking on a sidewalk, is it? It's a challenge because the sand or dirt isn't hard or packed down so it moves under your feet. If you try to climb a sand dune, you might even feel like you're slipping backward more than you're moving forward.

As you know, dromedary camels mainly live in the desert, but they have a much easier time than we do traveling on sand. This is because God created them with special pads on the bottom of their feet that flatten as they walk. The wider foot created by the pads provides extra stability. Think of it like the difference between walking in high heels and walking in snowshoes. Which one makes you steadier on your feet?

Sometimes life is compared to walking or a journey. Sometimes it's easy to get where we want to go, but other times it's hard and we think aren't making progress. When that happens, God wants us to know that He's with us and that He will help us to keep going.

The next time you see a camel:
Look at their feet and remember they can walk steadily, even in shifting sand. Also, remember that God helps us in our walk through life; He will steady us even when we don't think we can move forward.

Bible Verse

Proverbs 4:11-12

I guide you in the way of wisdom and lead you along straight paths. When you walk, your steps will not be hampered; when you run, you will not stumble.

Camel Hunt

To Do & Discover

Thousands of years ago, during ancient times, there were no cars, no phones and most families made or grew the things they needed. In Scripture, we can see that camels were very important in daily life and for people's survival.

What You Need:

A Bible

A Concordance (either print or online version)

Pen and paper for your answers

What to Do:

See how many times you can find camels mentioned in the Bible. Here are some questions and clues to get you started.

There are multiple answers to #1 & 2.

1. Find a verse where camels are listed as a part of someone's wealth or riches.

2. Find a passage where camels were used to help carry food or other belongings.

3. Who traveled by camel to meet her future husband? What was his name?

4. Which queen traveled in a camel caravan?

5. Find a passage that talks about someone wearing clothes made from camel hair.

Extra Fact:

When camels move, both legs on one side move forward at the same time. This means they cannot trot like a horse can.

Chameleon

What Do They Look Like?

There are over a hundred species of chameleons and they come in lots of shapes, sizes and colors. A few are teeny tiny and less than an inch long, but most grow to about twelve to eighteen inches when they're full size.

One thing they all have in common is the shape of their eyes. While most animals' eyes (and people's) sink into a space in the skull, chameleon eyelids are cone shaped and bump out from their face. Their pupil is a small opening at the very top. An even more unique feature is that each eye can move in almost any direction-and it doesn't matter what the other eye is doing! For example, if you want to look left, both eyes move that way, but for a chameleon one eye can look left, while the other can look right, front or sideways at the same time. As you might guess, this really helps them when they're looking for something to eat or for predators.

Most chameleons also have a prehensile tail, which means they can hang from it, and padded feet that help them grip tightly to tree branches.

Where Do They Live?

Chameleons can be found on several continents. They live on the islands of Madagascar and Hawaii, in India, Kenya, and Saudi Arabia. The kind of environment they like varies by species; some like it humid and cool, some live in the mountains and others where it's warm and dry.

What Do They Eat?

Most chameleons munch on insects like grasshoppers, and crickets. Occasionally, larger species may eat birds, too.

More Interesting Stuff

If you've seen crickets and grasshoppers you know they hop pretty fast, so you might think chameleons are fast too, but they're not - if they're using their legs, that is.

Chameleons catch prey with their super fast tongues, which they can flick in and out of their mouths about as fast as you can blink. The tongue is super long and the end of it is super sticky. These features allow them to easily catch fast hopping insects.

Chameleons are most famous for their ability to change the color of their skin. The belief that they can change to match anything they stand next to is a myth, however. Most of the time, chameleons are green or brown which camouflages them to their surroundings. Most of their other, brighter color changes reflect moods like angry or scared.

A New View

Chameleons use their ability to blend in with their surroundings in order to protect themselves. If they don't stand out, they hopefully won't become another animal's lunch. Did you know that people sometimes blend into their surroundings to protect themselves too? Of course, people don't change colors, but they do change other characteristics to avoid standing out.

For example, have you ever heard someone use language that's not nice around friends, when they speak much differently at home or at church? Kids (and adults) act that way because they don't want to be different; they want to blend in just like the chameleon, because it seems to make life better.

The problem is, when Christians act this way, it's not to protect ourselves from true danger. What we're usually afraid of is being teased or left out because the rest of the world doesn't agree with or understand our faith. Fact is, sometimes we're going to stand out if we follow God. Sometimes it can be a little scary, so we need to ask Him to help us stay strong and to keep Him first in our lives.

The next time you see a chameleon:

Remember God doesn't want us to blend into the world and do everything everyone else does. Instead, He wants us to be witnesses of our faith and His love for us so that others may come to know Him, too.

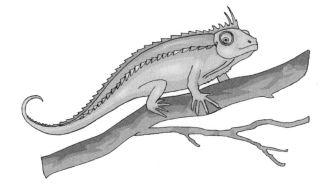

Bible Verse

Romans 12:2

Do not conform any longer to the pattern of this world, but be transformed by the renewing of your mind. Then you will be able to test and approve what God's will is—his good, pleasing and perfect will.

Quick Like Lightning

To Do & Discover

Chameleons are known for their lightning fast tongues. They can react in a matter of a split second to grab a snack. Let's see how you speedy you can be!

What You Need:

A deck of playing cards

Up to 3 people to play with

Extra Fact:

Chameleons use color changes to communicate with others. For example, if a female isn't interested in a male, she can change to a color that means "go away!"

What to Do:

You may know this game as "slap jack". Here are the rules if you've forgotten or have never played before.

1. Sit facing each other around a table or on the floor.

2. Deal all of the cards evenly, face down in front of each person. As you get your cards, put them into an even stack.

3. Decide who goes first. That person turns over one card to a discard pile in the middle of the table that everyone can reach. Turn it over so everyone sees it at the same time. Do not turn it towards you first.

4. Do this one person and one card at a time until someone turns up a Jack. When that happens, you want to try to be the first to slap your hand down on top of the pile. This is where you're going to test your speediness!

5. Whoever slaps the Jack gets to pick up and keep the whole pile of cards underneath. The object of the game is to collect cards and not run out.

6. If someone slaps a card that is not a Jack by mistake, he must give one card from his hand to the player who played the card that caused the slap.

7. If someone is out of cards, he can play the next round in case a Jack comes up and he can get cards again by taking the pile. If not, he is out. The last person with cards wins.

Flamingo

What Do They Look Like?

Flamingos are definitely easy to spot. They are not camouflaged to fit in with their surroundings at all. Most are cotton candy pink and some have scarlet feathers too. Flamingos also live in big groups, which makes it pretty much impossible to miss them. Also, imagine this: in one place where they live, there have been as many as a million birds all hanging out together in one big flock. Now that's a lot of pink!

Flamingos also have unique black-tipped beaks that curve under like a hook. They use their beaks to scoop up mud and filter out everything but the things they want to eat. They also have long, skinny legs and webbed feet that make it easy for them to wade in water. Sometimes they can walk where other birds and animals can't go.

Where Do They Live?

Flamingos live on several continents. South America and the eastern coast of Africa have some of the biggest populations.

Their main habitats are shallow lakes and lagoons. Often, these places don't have a lot of vegetation, so there aren't many other animals or birds that like to live there.

What Do They Eat?

Flamingos have a very special diet. They may not die without their special food, but if they don't eat it, they won't be pink!

Adult flamingos get their pink color from eating brine flies, shrimp and certain kinds of algae. These foods have beta-carotene in them. You may also know that carrots have beta-carotene in them too, but carrots don't grow where flamingos live.

If flamingos don't eat the right amount of these types of foods, they will start to lose their color and become pale. One exception to this is baby flamingos. Young birds are gray when they're born and do not start turning pink until they are about two years old.

More Interesting Stuff

Flamingos are very social birds. They like to do lots of things together as a group. For example, they often move together in the same direction. They can even turn, go a new way and stay together, just like a marching band or military squad.

A New View

You may have heard this from your parents or grandparents: you are what you eat. But what are they trying to tell you? Does it mean if you eat a cookie or a carrot your skin will turn orange or you'll grow chocolate freckles? No, of course not, thank goodness!

However, what we choose to eat is very important. For example, if we eat only unhealthy things, we probably won't feel well and we won't have a lot of energy. However, if we eat nutritious food, we'll grow strong, and our brains and bodies work better.

It's the same with our Christian life. We need to be fed with spiritual food regularly or we'll be weak and not the best we can be. That means going to church, taking communion and reading the Bible as often as we can.

The next time you see a flamingo:
Look at how pink they are and remember that they need to eat the right food in order to stay this way.

Think about how God provides spiritual food for his people, but it is up to us to make sure we get enough.

Bible Verse

Jeremiah 15:16

When your words came,
I ate them; they were my joy
and my heart's delight,
for I bear your name,

O LORD God Almighty.

A Lasting Impression

To Do & Discover

Even though people don't change colors because of what we eat, some foods do leave a lasting impression. Usually we call this a stain, but stains aren't always completely bad.

Have you ever eaten something that made your tongue, lips or fingers turn colors? Maybe you ended up with blue teeth, green fingers or a bright pink tongue. You might look a bit silly for a few minutes, but silly can be fun, right?

What You Need:

Make a list of all of the foods you could eat that stain your mouth or fingers. Just in case you need a hint, think of things like Jello™, slushy drinks and cotton candy.

As you made your list, you probably noticed that most of the foods that cause stains don't come from nature. However, there are at least a couple that you can find in the produce section at the store. Once again, just in case, here's a hint: one starts with B, the other with P.

What to Do:

For a special treat, eat one of the foods on your list and see what happens. Be careful not to get any on your clothes.

How much do you have to eat to get the stain?

How long does it last?

Is it possible to clean it off and if so, is there more than one way?

Extra Fact:

Flamingos need to have a running start in order to get off the ground for flight. Also, they usually take off into the wind.

Giant Panda

What Do They Look Like?

Giant pandas are probably one of the most recognized creatures on the planet. They look a lot like other bears, but their unique black and white coloring makes them stand out from the rest. Males and females look alike except males are larger.

Where Do They Live?

If you wanted to see a giant panda in the wild, you'd have a tough time trying to do it. Unfortunately, there are few giant pandas left in the world that do not live in a zoo. Scientists estimate that there are less than 1,000 still in the wild.

Those that have managed to survive live way up high in forest-covered mountains, in one tiny area of southwest China. They also spend a lot of time alone, so even if you knew where to look, it's a lot like trying to find a needle in a haystack.

What Do They Eat?

Think of one of your favorite foods. Got it? Now, think about eating that food for breakfast, lunch and dinner, almost every day, all year long. That's what mealtime is like for giant pandas.

Giant pandas eat bamboo and little else. Occasionally they'll eat other plants or a small mammal, but 99% of the time, they eat bamboo. They need to eat so much of it because each piece only has a little bit of the nutrients they need.

Unfortunately, having such a specialized diet is one of the reasons giant pandas are endangered. As people cut down more and more of the forests where they live, the pandas' food supply is getting smaller and smaller. It's also difficult for them to move to where the food is because people have built roads and buildings in the way. Pandas are very shy and they don't like to venture near these new things.

More Interesting Stuff

When they are born, giant pandas are anything but giant. Even though mom and dad weigh a couple hundred pounds, babies weigh four or five ounces at birth. That's about the size of a candy bar! They're also born without hair and they don't open their eyes for several weeks. Panda mothers gently hold their tiny babies in their paws and make sure they're okay, just like human moms do.

A New View

Have you ever noticed that it's easy to recognize and identify most black and white animals? Zebras, skunks, and of course giant pandas, aren't confused with other animals too often, if ever. You don't look at a panda and wonder if it might be a grizzly bear instead; whenever you see one, you know what it is.

Did you know that God wants Christians to be like giant pandas? When we interact with other people, He wants them to clearly know who and what we are - His children.

Can other people look at us and know that we're Christian? Sometimes they can, when we wear clothes or jewelry that have Christian symbols like a cross, and that's good, but God wants more.

He wants people to be able to tell we're Christians by how we talk, how we act, and how we treat others. For example, if everyone around us is picking on a classmate, we need to say something nice, or not participate at all. If it's time to pick a movie or a video game, our choices can let people know we are trying to follow God's word, too.

The next time you see a giant panda:
Remember how easy it is to recognize them and how God wants it to be just as easy for people to know we're His children.

Bible Verses

John 13:35

By this all men will know that you are my disciples, if you love one another."

John 15:8

This is to my Father's glory, that you bear much fruit, showing yourselves to be my disciples.

A Giant Reminder

To Do & Discover

There's lots of stuff you need to remember every day isn't there? There are things at school like answers to tests, and different things at home such as whose turn it is to do chores. It's easy to forget some of it, isn't it?

Here's a "giant" reminder to help you remember to live your life so that people can easily recognize that you are a child of God.

What You Need:

2 large white craft pompoms 2 to 2 ½ inch size

7 small black craft pompoms 1" size

1 small white craft pompom   ¾" size

Small piece of black felt or cloth or a black marker

Plastic eyes or cloth to cut some out

Glue (hot glue or craft glue is best if it is available)

   *If you don't have and don't want to buy individual pompoms,
     you can use a panda bear kit that you find at a craft store or online.

What to Do:

1. Glue the two large pompoms together, smaller one on top. Let them dry a little before moving on.

2. Glue on the small black pompoms for ears, legs, arms and tail.

3. Glue on small white pompom for snout.

4. Cut out tiny circle of black felt for the nose, glue on front of white pompom. If you don't have felt, use a permanent black marker to color in a black circle.

5. Glue on eyes.

6. Once your giant panda is dry, set it in a place where everyone can see it so that it can be your giant reminder!

Extra Fact:

Pandas are able to do somersaults and seem to enjoy doing them. Can you do a somersault?

Gorilla

What Do They Look Like?

What gorillas look like varies a little depending on where they live. Lowland gorillas have shorter, fine fur because they live in warm, humid forests or swampy areas. In comparison, mountain gorillas have thicker hair that's also a little longer because it gets much colder in the higher altitudes where they live. Their fur color is generally brownish gray to dark black.

One unique characteristic for males is that, as they get older (at least ten years old), some of the fur on their backs turns silvery gray. Normally, there is only one silverback in any family group. The rest are females and black back males.

Unlike some animals that are hairy all over, gorillas do not have hair on their faces, on the palms of their hands or soles of their feet; those parts show their blackish gray skin.

Where Do They Live?

Wild gorillas live in a small section of central Africa near the equator and that's it. They cannot be found anywhere else unless they're in a zoo. They're divided into two species – western and eastern, depending on where they live. They are also divided into lowland and mountain groups. Mountain gorillas are rare and can live at altitudes of several thousand feet. Lowland gorillas that live in the forests and marshes below are greater in number, but they're still endangered.

What Do They Eat?

Gorillas spend most of their day either eating or sleeping. They are mainly herbivores and eat lots of different fruits, plants, and roots and vines. Large adult males can eat thirty or forty pounds of food every day - that's like a person eating forty cans of vegetables or eighty apples!

More Interesting Stuff

Mature males, the silverbacks, have a lot of responsibilities once they form a family group, which is called a troop. First of all, they're in charge of deciding just about everything: which way the troop will travel for the day, where they'll stop to eat and when they'll rest. They also make sure the troop is safe and will do their best to defend it against any attackers.

One of silverback's other jobs is fairly unique in the animal world - they are mediators. If there's a problem or a fight between other members of the troop, the silverback will often step in to settle things down, decide who wins and put an end to the squabble.

A New View

Have you ever gone camping and stayed in a tent? If you haven't done that, have you ever pretended to have a tent or camp out in your living room? Either way, one of the things you had to do was set up camp. If you used a tent, it probably took a fair amount of effort to get everything set just right.

Now, imagine if you had to do that every night, or even if you wanted to take a quick nap in the afternoon. That's the life of a gorilla. As they travel to a new place to find food every day, each night they must build a new nest. They pull branches and leaves around them in their own version of setting up camp.

In the Old Testament, we can read about a group of people who also had to set up camp and put up a lot of tents. As the Israelites traveled on the way to the Promised Land, they set up and took down camp a lot. Sometimes they moved once a week, sometimes after being someplace just one day. Unlike gorillas though, they weren't moving to find food; they were learning how to trust and obey God's commands. When God said it was time to move, they needed to do it, whether they were happy about it or not.

The next time you see a gorilla:
Remember that they travel and build nests every night (gorilla camping) and how God used camping to teach the Israelites how to trust and obey Him.

Bible Verses

Exodus 19:1-2

In the third month after the Israelites left Egypt— on the very day—they came to the Desert of Sinai. After they set out from Rephidim, they entered the Desert of Sinai, and Israel camped there in the desert in front of the mountain.

Numbers 9:18

At the Lord's command the Israelites set out, and at his command they encamped. As long as the cloud stayed over the tabernacle, they remained in camp.

One of a Kind

To Do & Discover

It's very difficult to tell gorillas apart from each other. Unlike many other animals, they don't have spots or patches of color to set them apart. There is one way to figure it out, though - the nose knows. Every gorilla has a distinct nose; no two are the same. You have something on your body that is unique only to you too. Do you know what it is? Let's find out.

What You Need:

Ink pad or washable markers

Paper

Paper towels or a rag

A few friends or family members to do this with you

Extra Fact:

Gorillas sometimes use tools like we do. They may use rocks to smash open nuts or wave branches to scare off intruders.

What to Do:

1. Make sure your hands are clean and dry, especially your fingers.

2. Touch one fingertip to the ink pad or lightly rub the marker over it.

3. Press your finger slowly and firmly on the paper to try to get a clear finger print.

4. Clean off that finger, repeat for as many fingers as you want to do. Make the prints in a row on the paper and write which finger it is above the print. Also, put your name on the page.

5. If you are having trouble getting a good print by yourself, have someone else hold your finger steady, put the left edge down first and roll to the right.

6. There are eight basic finger print patterns, but every human's combination is one of a kind. Compare your fingerprints to the others in your group. How are they similar, how are they different?

7. It's a good idea to have a copy of everyone's fingerprints in case of an emergency. You can keep the ones you've made today or find out if your local police department has a special kit you can use instead.

Hippopotamus

What Do They Look Like?

There are only two land mammals that are bigger than hippos - elephants and rhinos (depending on the species). Hippos grow ten feet long or more, and full size males can weigh two or three tons. That's as heavy as two small cars!

In comparison to their huge size, some of their other features are small. They have a thin, wispy tail, small ears and short legs.

One other feature that's not so small is a hippo's mouth. They have wide, powerful jaws and long canine teeth that they can easily defend themselves with.

Where Do They Live?

Unless you live in certain parts of Africa, you don't have to worry about hippos showing up in your backyard.

In the wild, hippos only live in a handful of countries on the African continent. They live in and around rivers, lakes and even watering holes if they are deep enough. Moms even give birth and babies nurse underwater!

What Do They Eat?

Even though they have huge front teeth, hippos are plant and fruit eaters. In many ways, they're a live version of a lawnmower because they like to eat grass the most. They spend several hours grazing on land each evening once the sun goes down. During the day, it's back to the water.

More Interesting Stuff

The name "hippopotamus" comes from combining two Greek words and means "water horse". While they aren't even related to horses at all, the "water" part definitely fits.

If hippos aren't on land feeding, they're in the water. It is important for them to stay in the water, because they can dehydrate if their skin is in the sun too long. Sometimes they submerge only part way. When they do this, birds land on them thinking they're some sort of island. It must be an interesting sight when the birds figure out that the their landing spot doesn't stay in one place!

Hippos can also go completely under water because they can easily hold their breath for several minutes. Interestingly, they aren't true swimmers; instead, they bounce off the bottom, float a little, sink down and then push off again.

A New View

As hippos travel from water to land and back again they frequently take the same paths. Day after day, year after year, they walk on the plants along the way, crushing them down under their heavy footsteps.

At first, you might think this is a bad thing. After all, they're definitely damaging and may even kill some of the plants. However, the opposite is actually true.

As hippos create well-worn paths through the brush, they make it easier for smaller animals to get through. Think about it this way: if you were a little creature, you'd have a lot harder time making your way through tangled brush or long grass than a hippo. Once the hippos did their part though, the path would be clearer, safer and it would be easier to see where to walk.

As followers of Christ, we're in a similar situation as that small creature. God knows the best path for us. He leads the way and shows us the best way to go when we look to Him for guidance.

The next time you see a hippopotamus:
Remember how they create smooth pathways for other animals to travel. Think about how God wants to help us on life's road. Are you on His path or are you trying to clear the way yourself?

Bible Verses

Psalm 119:32

I run in the path of your
commands, for you have
set my heart free.

Psalm 18:36

You broaden the path
beneath me, so that
my ankles do not turn.

Sound Check

To Do & Discover

Many times when you see hippos at the zoo or on TV, they're hanging out in the water or grazing and they seem pretty quiet. However, in the wild, they actually communicate regularly with grunts, and other noises at various volumes. They can also hear sounds both above and below water.

What You Need:

Six or eight drinking glasses

Water

A pencil or wooden spoon

Extra Fact:

Even though hippos are huge, they can run up to 30 miles per hour. That means they can outrun you!

What to Do:

1. Line the glasses up in a row so there is a little space in between from one to the next.

2. Fill each glass with a different amount of water from almost empty to full.

3. Tap each glass with the pencil or spoon and see what kind of sound you get.

4. Which glass would you tap if you want a deep, low sound? Which one for a higher pitched noise?

5. Hippos communicate with different types of sounds and they all know what each sound pattern means. Using your glasses, tap out some sound patterns of your own and decide what they mean.

6. For example, the lowest and highest sound together might mean you're hungry, three others together might mean "come here."

7. Explain these patterns to someone, then play them and see if they can remember and identify what you're trying to say.

Red Kangaroo

What Do They Look Like?

Red kangaroos are the largest member of the kangaroo family. Males grow to between five and seven feet tall, which is taller than some adult people. True to their name, their coarse hair is reddish brown except for on their face and belly where it's white. Sometimes females are blue-gray instead of red and they aren't quite as tall as males.

At birth, red kangaroos look nothing like they do as adults. When they're born and make their way to their mom's pouch, they're hairless and barely bigger than a fingertip. During the next six months, they grow the familiar big feet, heavy tails and pointed ears of adult kangaroos. At that age, they're ready to leave the pouch and live with the rest of the adult group.

Where Do They Live?

Red kangaroos usually live in the dry plains or woodland areas of Australia. However, similar to the white-tailed deer in North America, red kangaroos are ablea to adapt to many environments and occasionally decide to live close to people in parks, gardens or other open areas of the suburbs.

What Do They Eat?

No matter where they live, red kangaroos are herbivores. Some eat lots of grass, others eat bigger plants and shrubs, but they mainly eat things that are low on the ground.

Red kangaroos also get a lot of the water they need from the plants they eat. If they can easily find water they'll drink it, if not, they're able to go without for several days. They are mostly active at night and rest during the hottest part of the day, which helps them to conserve water as well.

More Interesting Stuff

Imagine running a race and the faster you went, the easier it was to run. That's what it's like when a red kangaroo hops. They can actually go faster and faster until they reach their top speed without using hardly any extra energy at all. The springing motion of their leg and tail muscles creates exceptionally efficient movement. They don't usually need this endurance to outrun predators, but rather to cover large distances as they search for food.

Did you know kangaroos are the only large mammal that moves by hopping?

A New View

All mothers, whether they're animal or human, do some pretty awesome things for their families. For example, they work tirelessly to make sure everyone's fed, safe and healthy.

Kangaroo moms do all of these things too, but they also have a special ability that other animal moms don't have; they can provide two kinds of milk for their nursing young. They need to do this because they usually have two babies growing at different stages all the time. One baby in her pouch is a newborn that needs rich milk; another is six months to a year old and has started leaving the pouch from time to time. That one doesn't need the same kind of nutrition from its mom; it gets some solid food with the rest of the family.

As children of God, we are nourished by His word and we also are "fed" differently depending on how grown up we are in our faith life. Our parents, teachers and pastors work to make sure we have what we need at the right time.

The next time you see a kangaroo:
Remember how each baby gets a certain kind of food depending on what it needs and what it's ready for as it matures. Think about how we grow in faith and God's word in a similar way.

Bible Verse

1 Corinthians 3:1-2

Brothers, I could not address you as spiritual but as worldly—mere infants in Christ. I gave you milk, not solid food, for you were not yet ready for it. Indeed, you are still not ready.

Hop to It

To Do & Discover

When you think of something kangaroos are good at what do you think of? Jumping and hopping, of course! There are lots of things you can do that involve hopping and jumping too. How many can you think of? Video games do not count.

Here's a few to get things hoppin'.

What You Need:

You and a few friends or family members to play with

Depending on which activity you choose you may need:

Rope (can you guess what kind?)

A tape measure or yardstick and a paper and pen

Sidewalk chalk

Basketball hoop

Checkers or similar games

Extra Fact:

Kangaroos have lots of nicknames, males are sometimes called boomers, females jills and babies joeys.

What to Do:

1. **Jump Rope**
   See if you can do a few tricks like these: One jump but 2 spins of the rope, cross the rope in front, move forward while jumping. See how many times in a row you can jump using both feet.

2. **Try Hopscotch**
   Hopscotch is a very old game. Some of the earliest records of it are of Roman soldiers using it a training exercise for quick movement. There are a few different ways to play. Do a little research, pick one, draw the playing area on a sidewalk or driveway and challenge your friends.

3. **Have a Long Jump Contest**
   Find a patch of grass or see if you are allowed to use a jumping sand pit at a school. Mark a starting line, have a tape measure or yardstick ready. Jump! See how far you can go, record it on a sheet of paper. Give everyone a chance to try. Grownups too! See who can go the furthest or who can beat their first try by the most distance.

4. **Have a Jump Shot Contest**
   How many can you do in a row? How far away can you be and still make the shot? It doesn't matter if you play or want to play on a team or not, give it a try.

5. **Hop Inside**
   If the weather is bad, or you are unable to do the other activities, try a board game with lots of jumps like checkers, Chinese checkers or peg and holes puzzles.

King Penguin

What Do They Look Like?

King penguins can grow to about three feet tall and are the second tallest member of the penguin family. Only their relatives, emperor penguins, are bigger. In fact, sometimes people confuse the two because they look quite a bit alike.

One way to tell the difference between emperors and kings is by the markings on their head and neck. King penguins have an upside down tear drop shaped orange patch on each side of their head, while the emperor's patch is wider and mostly yellow. King penguins also have an orange area on their lower beaks that is much brighter than what emperors have.

If you happen to see young penguins, you'd also be able to tell the difference. Emperor penguin young are fluffy and gray with white faces. King babies are fuzzy too, but they are cocoa brown all over.

Where Do They Live?

Some people believe that all penguins live where there's snow and ice all the time, but that isn't true.

King penguins live on sub-Antarctic islands. This means they live on islands that are in the ocean between Antarctica and parts of South America, Africa and Australia. They live near or on the beach and most of the time, the ground is muddy or green with plant life.

What Do They Eat?

The menu of what king penguins like to eat is fairly small. They mainly feed on squid and several kinds of fish, including one called a lantern fish that glows in the dark!

More Interesting Stuff

You probably know that penguins cannot fly in the air like most birds. However, their wings propel them gracefully and quickly in the water. Many people say this is their version of flying.

Besides being strong swimmers, king penguins are some of the best, deepest divers of all the penguin species. They regularly dive a couple hundred feet down and can go more than 500 feet. Most people cannot dive that deep without being in some kind of submarine.

During the winter months, when the ground is snowy, king penguins are also really good at a technique called tobogganing. They slide on their bellies to get around. For them, it's much faster than walking or waddling.

A New View

Imagine this: You've been boating and on a lake with a friend on a sunny afternoon. Now it's time to rejoin your family. You get back to the beach and there are people as far as you can see in every direction! The beach is full of kids and families and you have no idea where your parents are. What would you do?

This is what life is like every day for king penguins. Moms and dads go out to sea to get food and when they come back, there are hundreds of hungry chicks waiting. And remember, they all look alike!

Luckily, penguin parents and chicks don't have to rely on sight to find each other. Instead, when a parent returns, they call out with a special sound that only their family knows. The chick responds with their own special whistle, they find each other, and the chick gets the food it needs.

The next time you see a king penguin:
Think about how parents and chicks know each other through their voices. Remember that God, our heavenly Father cares about us and wants us to talk to Him. He knows our voice and we should learn to know His too.

Bible Verse

Psalm 116:1

I love the LORD, for he heard my voice;
he heard my cry for mercy.

Dive In!

To Do & Discover

King penguins feed in the ocean. They're able dive and swim at many different depths to find fish and squid. This activity will help you learn a little more about diving.

What You Need:

A clear two-liter plastic bottle with cap

Plastic eyedropper

Water

Extra Fact:

King penguins are able to drink salty seawater. They have a special gland that removes the salt that they then get rid of through their nose!

What to Do:

You are making a Cartesian diver, named after the scientist René Descartes (pronounced renay daycart).

1. Fill the bottle with water up to the top.

2. Fill the eyedropper about halfway with water.

3. Carefully put the dropper into the bottle. You'll have to do it quickly; don't worry if you spill a little.

4. Put the cap on and make sure it's airtight, but you also may need to remove it, so keep that in mind and don't put it on too tight.

5. Squeeze the bottle & see what happens. If the diver doesn't move, you may need to adjust the seal or water level in the bottle.

6. Other items can be used as divers. Believe it or not, fast food condiment packets like ketchup usually work. Try it!

Lion

What Do They Look Like?

Most of you probably know what a lion looks like because you see often see them in books, on TV and in zoos. However, did you know lions are the only ones in the cat family where males and females look distinctly different from each other?

Male lions are known for their big, bushy manes; usually, the darker the mane, the older the lion is. Females don't have manes because they run a lot more than males; manes are heavy and they'd get too hot. It would be a lot like if you ran around wearing a heavy winter coat; you'd probably be pretty uncomfortable and unable to run for very long.

Where Do They Live?

Most lions live in Africa, but there is also one species that lives in a small part of India. African lions live on savannas and plains, wide-open places with lots of low grasses and a few trees.

What Do They Eat?

Lions are often called the "king of beasts." This is because they are at the top of the food chain in the areas where they live. They are large and powerful so they help to control the populations of other big animals that don't have many other predators.

Females should probably be called the "queen of beasts" because they actually do most of the hunting. Typically, several lionesses hunt together, and each one has a job. Some "herd" the prey towards the group while others catch it.

More Interesting Stuff

Unlike other large cats that prefer to be alone most of the time, lions live together in small family groups called "prides." Usually there are a few females, cubs and one or two males in a pride.

Members of a pride are very close to each other, just like many human families. They hunt and eat together and young ones play together. Baby lions can even get milk from any mom in the pride - sort of like going to a friend's house for dinner!

Lion life is often quite efficient because everyone pitches in. Females do most of the hunting, while the males are in charge of making sure the group is safe, especially the cubs, while the females are out looking for their next meal.

Even though lions are one of the most powerful hunters, they use their energy in short bursts. They spend the rest of their time sleeping and napping. When you add up the time in between activity, sometimes lions spend as many as 21 hours out of 24 just laying around!

A New View

When people think about lions, words like strength, majestic and courageous come to mind. They are considered royalty of the animal world.

The Bible often talks about royalty like kings, queens, pharaohs and princes. In the Old Testament, some were good, wise, and followed God's commands. Others created idols or believed they themselves were more important than God.

During this time, God's people were waiting for a new king, the Messiah. They believed he would rescue them and create a new kingdom on earth.

Thousands of years later, the Messiah Jesus did come, just as the prophets said. But he didn't create a new government; instead, He came to be king in our hearts and to prepare us to live in a heavenly kingdom some day.

The next time you see a lion: Think about your Lord Jesus Christ, the King of Kings, the ruler of heaven and earth. He loves you very much and someday he will welcome you into his heavenly kingdom where you will live in His glory forever.

Bible Verse

Luke 1:32-33

He will be great and will be called the Son of the Most High.
The Lord God will give him the throne of his father David,
and he will reign over the house of Jacob forever; his
kingdom will never end.

Lion of Pride

To Do & Discover

Lions live in groups called "prides." You are probably also familiar with another definition of pride which means "to be proud of." Even though too much pride or being arrogant is not a positive thing, it is okay for you to be proud of yourself (and others) when you accomplish something good, or just because you're God's special creation.

Here's something to help you remember to be proud in the good way.

What You Need:

1 brown, white or yellow lunch size bag

Construction paper-yellow and brown

Brown yarn

Markers, scissors, glue

Note: You may want to have enough supplies to make two or more.

Extra Fact:

Lions are the loudest of the big cats. In the calm of the night, their roars can be heard up to five miles away.

What to Do:

1. Lay bag on work surface with flap facing up (you're looking at it), back should be flat side.

2. Cut strips of construction paper (one or both colors) about ½ inch wide, 2 inches long. Glue them around the flap one at a time, sticking out for the mane.

3. Draw a face on the flap (eyes, nose, and whiskers).

4. Cut out circle about the size of a half dollar from the construction paper. Cut it in half. Glue one half on each side of the head near the top for ears.

5. Cut a piece of yarn about 6 - 8 inches long
   Fuzz/fray one end to make the tail tuft, glue the other end on back of the bag near the bottom.

6. When everything is thoroughly dried, carefully put your hand inside if you want to use your lion as a puppet. You can also stand it up by placing it over a large cup or mug.

7. When you see or play with your lion, remember to be proud of yourself.

8. You might also want to make more lions of pride to share with loved friends or family. Tell them you're proud of them too!

Orangutan

What Do They Look Like?

There are two species of orangutans, Sumatran and Bornean. You can easily tell orangutans apart from other apes and monkeys because they have bright red hair. Also, orangutans are generally only about three or four feet tall, but their arm span can be seven feet wide!

Adult male orangutans also have what are called "cheek pads", thick areas of skin on the sides of their faces. Females are smaller than males and do not have this feature.

Where Do They Live?

Orangutans only live in the wild in two small areas of the world, the islands of Sumatra and Borneo. They live high up in the trees of the rainforest and only come down to the ground if it's absolutely necessary. In fact, because their hands and feet are so useful for climbing and swinging, they don't work as well for walking.

Unfortunately, because their habitat is so small and more and more is destroyed every day, they could be extinct in the wild very soon.

What Do They Eat?

Orangutans really love fruit; in fact, they eat as many as 300 different kinds. Figs are just one of their favorites. They also like honey and nectar.

Even though you might think with 300 choices they'd never run out of things to eat, orangutans do a lot of searching through the forest to find their food. They have to learn which fruits are ripe and where they can be found each season of the year. Sometimes they even hang upside down to reach the particular fruit they want.

More Interesting Stuff

In the Malay language, the name "orangutan" means "man (or person) of the forest". They aren't really human of course, but there are some similarities between them and us. For example, if you see an orangutan sitting quietly and it seems to be staring off into space, it's very possible he's not bored; instead, he may be trying to solve a problem!

Scientists believe Orangutans to prefer to think things through slowly rather than quickly jumping from one idea to another. They have a keen sense of observation, which means they look at the challenge, and think it over carefully. The rarely try random answers to reach a solution and they often seem to figure out just what they need to do at just the right time.

A New View

Orangutans are the only animal whose offspring take many years to grow from child to adult. This is probably because they have so much to learn! Young ones stay with their moms to learn all they need to know to stay healthy and out of trouble.

Mothers show both male and female offspring which kinds of fruit are safe and good to eat. This is important because in the rainforests where they live, there are thousands of plants and other things to choose from. Females also learn how to care for the babies they'll have someday.

Orangutans are considered young and don't really grow up until they are teenagers, just like human kids. Once they are mature, males live by themselves most of the time so they must remember everything their moms taught them in order to survive.

The next time you see an orangutan:
Think about how much they are like you and how important it is for them to remember what they learn when they're young. Be thankful for the adults in your life who teach you the important things you need to know including how to live as a child of God.

Bible Verse

Proverbs 4:13

Hold on to instruction, do not let it go;
guard it well, for it is your life.

They Swing from the Trees with Greatest of Ease

To Do & Discover

Orangutans are born to swing and live in the trees. People aren't quite as good at it, but we have some of that ability too. If you've ever been told you're a little monkey, today you can show people why that can be a good thing.

What You Need:

A place where you can climb trees or a jungle gym.

Do not go by yourself. Make sure someone else is there to help keep you safe.

Think of all the activities orangutans do each day even though they are always high up in the treetops.

Make a list on a piece of paper you can take with you.

If your list includes eating (and it should) you might want to pack a little snack

Hint: There are three more clues about what you should put on your list in this chapter.

What to Do:

1. Pick a tree or find the jungle gym (they're also called monkey bars) you want to climb on.

2. Choose an activity from the list and try to do it as you think an orangutan would. For example, do you think you could eat a snack while sitting on the monkey bars or in a tree?

3. Don't forget one that we didn't talk about yet – play! Young orangutans especially like to swing, hang from branches and have fun together.

Enjoy being outside and feel free to "monkey around!"

Extra Fact:
Orangutans make a laughing sound if they're tickled!

Polar Bear

What Do They Look Like?

Polar bears are easily recognized because they are the only bears with white coats. Surprisingly, their hair isn't really white at all, it's clear and the strands are hollow. Reflection of sunlight is what makes them look white. Their outer layer of hair is very important because it helps to keep water away from their skin, and that helps keep them warm in the freezing cold ocean.

Polar bears also have large front paws that help them travel easily without slipping across ice and snow. They're also strong swimmers because their wide feet help propel them just like big paddles help a boat. In fact, their scientific name means "maritime bear."

They are also the largest members of the bear family and one of the biggest predators on earth. They can weigh over half a ton and grow to be ten feet long. That means when they stand upright, they may be taller than the ceilings in your house!

Where Do They Live?

Polar bears live in the Arctic Circle region at the tippy-top of the world. They can be found in Alaska in the U.S., the northern parts of Canada, Greenland, and Russia.

Sometimes you might read in a storybook or see in a cartoon that polar bears and penguins live together. In reality, that couldn't be further from the truth. They really live at opposite ends of the earth!

What Do They Eat?

Because Polar bears spend much of their lives on floating ice, they don't have a big menu to pick from. Seals are their most abundant food source. A polar bear can smell a seal (its favorite meal) from miles away. Wouldn't it be fun if you could smell your favorite meal cooking from way down the street?

More Interesting Stuff

Polar bears can also go weeks without eating if they need to and use the fat stored in their bodies for energy until they're able to hunt again.

You may also see a polar bear "take a bath" by rolling around on the snow to get clean.

A New View

Have you ever had to wait for something? I'm sure you have; we all do. We wait our turn in line, we wait for our birthday to come each year, and we wait for the light to change at an intersection.

Sometimes these things seem like they take FOREVER don't they? Often, we want them to go faster, to happen right now instead of later. Sometimes we even get upset when we think people are taking too long. We get impatient.

God tells us that when we have to wait, we need to try to wait patiently. Even when we ask Him for something in prayer, the answer doesn't always come right when we want it. Having patience is one of the ways we show our trust in Him and that He knows what's best for us.

The next time you see a polar bear:
Think about how patient they are even though they're hungry and tired. The next time you just can't wait for something to happen, ask God to help you to be patient too.

Bible Verses

Proverbs 14: 29

A patient man has great understanding, but a quick-tempered man displays folly.

Colossians 3:12

Therefore, as God's chosen people, holy and dearly loved, clothe yourselves with compassion, kindness, humility, gentleness and patience.

Going Out to Eat

To Do & Discover

Because of global warming, the ice the polar bears need to live on is melting faster than it ever has before, so now they must travel greater distances to find food. This activity will help you understand a little of what it's like for them at mealtime.

What You Need:

Choose a favorite snack that can be put into bowls or on little plates. Separate it into four small portions. For example, if the favorite snack is pretzels or grapes, put a few in four different bowls.

Extra Fact:

Unlike other animals that run fast and chase their prey, polar bears sit very still and wait, sometimes for hours, until a seal comes up for air through the ice. How long do you think you could sit and wait for your food when you're hungry?

What to Do:

1. Have a grownup put one snack portion in the kitchen.

2. Next, put one portion in a nearby room, then one farther away.

3. Place the last portion in the room farthest room from the kitchen (or maybe even all the way at a neighbor's house if they say it's okay).

4. When you're ready for snack time, go to the kitchen first because that's where food usually is right?

5. When you want more food, you have to go to the next room.

6. While you might be having fun at the moment, you probably wouldn't like to do this every time you wanted to eat-especially if all your food was at a neighbors house. By pitching in to help the environment, even if it's just a little, you might help the ice to stop melting so polar bears have an easier time finding the food they need.

Prairie Dog

What Do They Look Like?

Even though their name is prairie dog, this animal isn't a dog at all. They're actually in the rodent family, specifically, a type of squirrel. They got their name because of the bark like sound they make when they're scared.

There are several species of prairie dogs, but most of them look about the same. They're tan with white bellies, a little over a foot long and they weigh about two or three pounds.

Where Do They Live?

As you might have guessed, prairie dogs live on prairies. Prairies are large areas of grassland habitat such as the Great Plains in the United States. Prairie dogs can be found in the prairie lands from Canada to Mexico. However, their habitat is shrinking because people are now using a lot of the land where they used to live for farms and towns.

What Do They Eat?

Prairie dogs are herbivores. They munch on a variety of leafy plants, seeds and roots.

You might consider them the "lawn mowers" of the prairie because their feeding habits help keep plants under control. They even control the plants they don't like to eat by gnawing them down short with their teeth.

More Interesting Stuff

Imagine a large city with lots of people moving around, going to work and getting together to visit. Now imagine this city being underground, and you'll have a good idea about what prairie dog communities are like.

These communities are called colonies or towns and may contain hundreds or even thousands of prairie dogs. Also, within the colonies are smaller family groups called coteries (pronounced coe-tur-ees).

Prairie dog life is similar to ours in several ways. First, they all have jobs to do each day like hunting for food or keeping the burrows in repair. In addition, their burrows have separate areas for sleeping and raising young very much like the rooms in your home. There's even one that's a bathroom!

A New View

One of the most important jobs for the prairie dog colony is sentry or guard. There is always at least one member of the colony standing watch and looking for predators. If danger is spotted, the first one to see it signals the rest of the group by barking, and by jumping or bobbing up and down. It drops into the tunnels for safety if the predator gets too close.

If a predator continues to move through the colony, other members will try to alert the others as to where it is and where it's going. Everyone works to help keep the whole community safe.

As members of the family of God, we also need to look out for those around us. If we believe someone is in danger, whether physically or spiritually, we need to warn them and try to keep them from getting hurt.

The next time you see a prairie dog:
Think about how their communities are a lot like ours and how they work together and protect each other. Think about who you need to help protect in your family or group of friends.

Bible Verse

1 Peter 5:8

Be self-controlled and alert. Your enemy the devil prowls around like a roaring lion looking for someone to devour.

Safe & Sound

To Do & Discover

Luckily, we don't have to worry about hawks, owls and coyotes like prairie dogs do. However, there are still lots of things in our homes that can cause harm if we aren't careful. However, just like the prairie dogs, there's lots of help around to keep us safe too.

What You Need:

A piece of paper and something to write with

An adult to do this with you

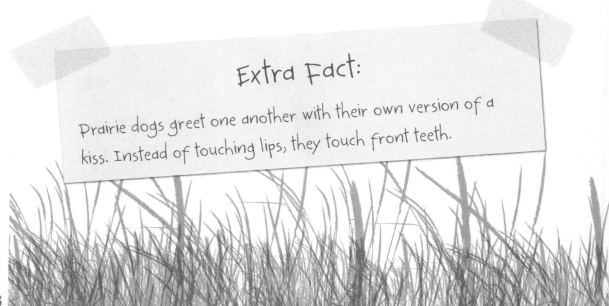

Extra Fact:

Prairie dogs greet one another with their own version of a kiss. Instead of touching lips, they touch front teeth.

What to Do:

1. Draw a line dividing the piece of paper in half from top to bottom.

2. At the top of the first column, write "Danger", on the other one write "What Keeps Us Safe."

3. Walk through your house (and your yard if you'd like) with an adult. Look for things that are dangerous and write them in the first column. In the second column, write down what protects you from that danger.

4. For example, in the first column you might write "stove" in the second column you could write, "not touching it or making sure it is off."

5. Besides the ones you can see, list types of danger that you can't see right now. Fire and carbon monoxide are just two examples.

6. Once you've made your list, share it with your family and friends to help them stay safe too.

Pronghorn

What Do They Look Like?

Can you name an animal that has horns? Can you name an animal that has antlers? Now, can you name an animal that has hornlers, or how about antlorns?

What? You mean you've never heard of those? That's okay; it was a bit of a trick question. Those words don't really exist, though maybe they should. If you wanted a word for the growths on a pronghorn's head, these words would actually fit because they have neither true horns nor true antlers. Instead, they have a combination of both. They are referred to as horns, but they are shed each year and have prongs or forks like antlers. No other animal in the world has these kinds of horns.

Pronghorns get their name from the shape of their horns. Sometimes they're also called American antelopes because they look like the antelopes of Africa. Pronghorns also resemble small deer, but they aren't close relatives.

Where Do They Live?

Pronghorns live in the wide open prairies and deserts of North America. They are fairly common and can be found in Nevada, Arizona, parts of Texas, California, Canada and northern Mexico.

What Do They Eat?

In spring and summer, a wide variety of juicy flowering plants, bushes, grass and even cactus make good meals for a hungry pronghorn. When the weather is hot and dry, and during winter, they'll also eat harder, woody stemmed plants.

More Interesting Stuff

While cheetahs are known as the fastest land mammal, pronghorns are a close second place. They are considered the fastest mammal of North America. Pronghorns also have an advantage over cheetahs because they can run for a few miles at high speed instead of only half a mile or so. Another way to look at it is pronghorns are like sports cars; they can run for at least a few miles at a time compared to drag racing cars that only go a few yards or a quarter mile at a time (like cheetahs). As long as a pronghorn is healthy, this endurance enables them to outrun virtually any predator.

Besides having speed and endurance to help them stay safe from danger, pronghorns also have very large eyes and excellent sight. As they look across the flat prairie land, they can see movement up to three miles away! People need to use binoculars to even come close to that kind of range of vision.

A New View

There's no doubt that a healthy adult pronghorn can outrun its enemies. This being the case, you might think that if one got scared, it would just take off running and keep going until it was safe. You might be surprised to learn that this isn't what happens most of the time.

Unlike some animals that live alone most of their lives, pronghorns live in herds. This means they're rarely far away from other members of the group. If one of them senses danger, the first thing it tries to do is signal the rest, even though it could run away and only worry about itself. The other individuals do not scatter in all directions either. Instead, they all begin to run together, usually in an oval shaped formation similar to how birds fly in flocks. This confuses predators and makes it hard for them to focus on one animal to attack. Even though each pronghorn could be pretty safe on its own, it knows it's even safer in that group.

The next time you see a pronghorn:
Think about how they protect each other and how they're even more fearless against their enemies as a group. Also, remember that God doesn't bring us to faith and then expect us to survive alone. He encourages Christians to meet together regularly with others so that we can support each other and be strong against our troubles and enemies.

Bible Verse

Hebrews 10:24-25

And let us consider how we may spur one another on toward love and good deeds. Let us not give up meeting together, as some are in the habit of doing, but let us encourage one another—and all the more as you see the Day approaching.

Hiding in Plain Site

To Do & Discover

For the first few months after they're born, baby pronghorns have to hide to avoid predators. They sit as still as possible in the tall brown grass which camouflages them.

What You Need:

You (the hider)

Friends and family (searchers)

Four or five objects (or more if you'd like) about the size of a tennis ball, not too big, not too small. Also, it's best if they're a solid color. For example, an apple is solid red.

A piece of paper and a pen for each person who is a searcher

Extra Fact:

If you sing the song "Home on the Range" you'll be singing about pronghorns - remember they're also called antelope.

What to Do:

Baby pronghorns can hide in the middle of wide open spaces because they blend into their surroundings. In this game, your job is to hide objects in plain site, so that the searchers don't notice them right away or never find them at all.

1. Let everyone know what objects will be hidden. You can make it more challenging if you tell them but don't show them what they are. However, you must be specific enough so that they clearly understand what they're looking for.

2. Have all searchers close their eyes and stay in one area while the hider hides each object.

3. Hide the objects by:
    a) Trying to camouflage them. Example: hiding a green ball in green plants.
    b) Putting them in a place where they blend in/look natural. Example: a piece of plastic fruit in a bowl that's normally on the table filled with real fruit.

4. Set a time limit. As searchers find objects, have them write down what it is and where they found it, preferably without telling anyone else.

5. When time is up, the person who finds the most objects wins. To be fair, finding something extra that is similar does not count. It must be the exact object that was hidden.

Ring-tailed Lemur

What Do They Look Like?

Many animals are easily identified through special markings, often these markings are black and white. Think of pandas, zebras and skunks. Ring-tailed lemurs are in this group too. Their special markings, as their name says, are on their tails. The stacked black and white rings are hard to miss and make it easy to know which animal you're looking at.

And if by chance you cannot see their tail, you'd still see rings - they also have one around each eye. You'll also notice their eyes are yellow or orange, not blue or brown like people's are. The rest of their face and ears are tufted white and the rest of their body is a soft gray or brown.

Where Do They Live?

In the wild, most species of lemurs, including the ring-tailed, live on the island of Madagascar. It's a very tiny place compared to most other countries, and unfortunately, lemur habitat is getting smaller and smaller every day.

The forests they need to live are being destroyed so that farms and crops can be put there instead. Hopefully, people will figure out a way to compromise soon so that lemurs continue to have a place to live, too.

What Do They Eat?

Fruits, leaves, flowers and berries are high on the list of things ring-tailed lemurs like to eat. The tamarind plant is their favorite. Believe it or not, they also think tree sap is a tasty treat.

More Interesting Stuff

Unlike most lemur species, ring-taileds spend a lot of time on the ground instead of in the treetops. One of their favorite things to do when they're on the ground is to soak up the sunshine.

The can often be found sitting on a rock, feet and paws stretched out wide, so that as much of their body as possible can feel the warm rays. They close their eyes too, which sort of makes them look like they're doing lemur yoga! While sunbathing can be harmful for people, scientists believe it helps lemurs stay warm when the forest gets chilly later in the evening.

A New View

If you've ever gone for a hike in the woods with a group of friends, you probably chose someone to be the leader. That person walked ahead and either made a path through, or found a way to get where you wanted to go. The rest of you would have tried to keep your eyes on that person, so that you knew which way to walk.

Ring-tailed lemurs do this too. Whenever they walk together as a group, there's always a leader. It holds its tail high in the air like a flag. The others keep that tail in sight so they don't get lost and so they know which way to go.

In the Bible, we can read about another group that did a lot of walking and a lot of following. The Israelites walked for many years until they finally reached the Promised Land. During part of that time, they had the unique experience of being able to see and follow God himself! He appeared in a cloud and as fire in the sky moving ahead of them to lead the way. Imagine what that would have been like. Wouldn't it be wonderful if we could do that today?

The next time you see a ring-tailed lemur:
Look at that fluffy ringed tail. Maybe you'll be lucky enough to see them lead each other around. Remember the special way that God lead the Israelites and how confident they could be in His faithfulness to guide them in the ways they needed to go.

Bible Verse

Exodus 13:20-22

After leaving Succoth they camped at Etham on the edge of the desert. By day the LORD went ahead of them in a pillar of cloud to guide them on their way and by night in a pillar of fire to give them light, so that they could travel by day or night. Neither the pillar of cloud by day nor the pillar of fire by night left its place in front of the people.

Let the Son Shine In

To Do & Discover

We know ring-tailed lemurs love the s-u-n; now let's talk about the S-o-n we love, Jesus Christ.

What You Need:

A Bible

A paper and pencil to write down your answers

Try this yourself then challenge your friends and family members to see if they can do it!

Extra Fact:

Lemurs cannot hang from their tails like other primates can.

What to Do:

See how many of these verses you can complete without having to look them up. If you have some left over, there are hints to help you the rest of the way. If it's easy for you to fill in the blanks, see if you can give the chapter and verse too.

1. And she gave birth to her firstborn, a son. She wrapped him in cloths and placed him in a _____ because there was no room for them in the inn. (Hint: Luke)

2. While he was still speaking, a bright cloud enveloped them, and a voice from the cloud said, "This is my Son, whom I love; with him I am _____ _____. Listen to him!" (Hint: Matthew)

3. You are all sons of God through _____ in Christ Jesus (Hint: Galations)

4. This is _____: not that we ____ God, but that he _____ us and sent his Son as an atoning sacrifice for our sins. (Hint: 1 John)

5. He will be _____ and will be called the Son of the _____ _____. The Lord God will give him the throne of his father David (Hint: Luke)

6. And when the centurion, who stood there in front of Jesus, heard his cry and saw how he _____, he said, "Surely this man was the ____ ____ ____!" (Hint: Mark)

Sea Star

What Do They Look Like?

Many people know sea stars as starfish, but marine scientists would like to change that because they really aren't fish. They're actually related to sand dollars and sea cucumbers. Did you know there are at least 1,800 different kinds of sea stars?

Sea stars can be as small as a quarter and as big as three feet across. They also come in just about every color of the rainbow. Some of them have cool names like Chocolate-Chip Sea Star and Necklace Sea Star.

Sea stars are invertebrates, which means their skeletons are on the outside of their body (compared to your skeleton being on the inside). Sea stars usually have hard spikes or bumps all over their top side too. They also have hundreds of suction cup feet on their bottom side that help them grip food and to move around.

Most species of sea stars have five arms that grow from the center of their body. This creates their star shape. However, they don't always have five arms; they can have ten, twenty and sometimes more!

Where Do They Live?

Sea stars live the ocean. There aren't any that live in fresh water. Some live on reefs, some deep on the bottom. If you go to the ocean, you might be able to see one, because some live in shallow areas and tide pools near the beach.

What Do They Eat?

Sea stars mainly like to eat things with shells such as oysters, clams or snails. Sometimes they eat tiny plankton and coral too. Knowing what sea stars eat is only half of the story though; understanding how they eat it is the really interesting part.

Unlike most animals (and people) that get food to their stomach through their mouths, sea stars send their stomach out to get it! As strange as it sounds, sea stars have two stomachs and they can push one of them part way out of their body and into the shells of their prey to start digesting it. Later, they pull everything back in and pass the partially eaten food to their second stomach to finish it.

More Interesting Stuff

Sea stars generally don't move too fast and use they their suction cup feet to creep around. They can also hold on really tight to rocks while waves crash over them so they don't float away.

A New View

The Bible talks about stars in several different places. In Genesis, we learn God made the sun, moon, and stars. God also told Abram that he would have as many descendents as there are stars in the sky. But probably the most famous star in the Bible is the one the wise men (also called Magi) followed to find the baby Jesus.

Back in those days, there were no computers so they didn't have GPS to help them find their way.

Instead, God gave them a big, bright star so they wouldn't miss it. The wise men followed that star until they reached their destination. There they saw God's greatest Christmas gift to us – the baby Jesus.

The next time you see a sea star:

Remember how God used a star to lead the wise men on their journey to see the Christ child. Think about how He's leading you in your life now and where He wants you to go for Him.

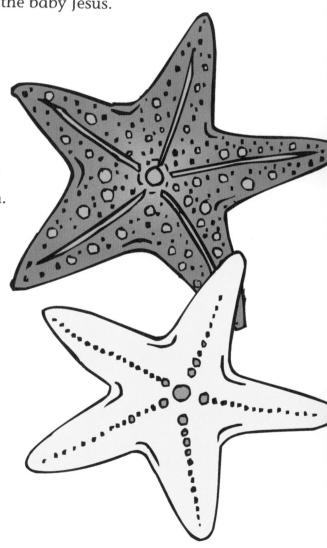

Bible Verse

Matthew 2: 9-11

After they had heard the king, they went on their way, and the star they had seen in the east went ahead of them until it stopped over the place where the child was. When they saw the star, they were overjoyed. On coming to the house, they saw the child with his mother Mary, and they bowed down and worshiped him.

She Sees Sea Stars on the Seashore

To Do & Discover

When people think of sea stars, they often think of the brown, dried kind you might find at the beach or at a souvenir store. But you know that's not what they look like when they're alive right? Let's see what kind of beautiful sea star you can make.

What You Need:

Construction paper or heavy drawing paper

(white or colored)

Crayons or markers, scissors

White glue

One or more texture item: sand, glitter, sequins, rice or dried peas.

A 9 or 10 inch Paper plate

What to Do:

1. Draw a sea star about as big as an adult hand. Most have 5 arms, but you can add more if you like. If you are using white paper and you'd like to color your sea star, do that now.

2. Carefully cut it out.

3. Spread a thin layer of glue on one arm. Lightly sprinkle on a texture item. Continue section by section until you've added as much texture as you like. Shake excess off and discard. Let dry thoroughly.

4. Create a place for your sea star to live by coloring the plate to look like the bottom of the ocean, or rocks by a beach.

Extra Fact:

Sea stars don't have brains. Also, the liquid in their bodies is seawater; they don't have any blood at all.

Tapir

(pronounced tay-per)

What Do They Look Like?

The first time you see a tapir you might guess it's some kind of pig, or maybe an anteater, but they are neither of these and they aren't even related to them at all. They're actually relatives of horses and rhinos.

Tapirs aren't huge animals by comparison and only grow to be five to six feet long. They also have short tails and legs and small ears. They generally weigh 500 to 800 pounds.

Three of the four tapir species are plain brown or black in color, however Malayan Tapirs are a little different. Their front and rear end are black, but their middle is white, making it look like they're wearing a saddle. This helps them blend into the dark jungle and makes it harder for predators to see them in the shadows of the forest.

Another thing you'll notice is that tapirs have a unique looking nose, which is called a proboscis. It's soft, flexible and the nostrils are at the end. They use it to pick leaves and grasp things much like an elephant uses its trunk.

Where Do They Live?

 Most species of tapirs can be found in Mexico, Central America, and in several countries in South America as well. Some of them live high in chilly mountain forests; others live where it's warm and humid for most of the year. Malayan Tapirs are the only species that can be found in Asia. They live in small areas of Malaysia, Thailand and Indonesia. Rainforests are their primary habitat.

What Do They Eat?

Tapirs are plant eaters. They look for tender leaves, buds and branches on low growing plants. Fallen fruit is a tasty treat too. They rely on that flexible nose and a sensitive sense of smell to find their food because they mainly eat at night.

Tapirs that live in warmer climates also like to spend time in rivers and ponds. As they keep themselves cool, they enjoy eating many types of aquatic vegetation too.

More Interesting Stuff

Tapirs seek shelter and sleep a lot during the day. This helps them avoid predators that hunt during daylight hours. In addition, even though they don't have long legs, tapirs can run rather quickly when they need to. If there's a pond or river nearby, they'll also run right into the water to hide!

A New View

Sometimes when people first see a tapir, they think it's a very strange creature. They don't recognize it and don't understand how it fits in with other animals they're more familiar with. They may even be a little afraid.

However, if they take the time to learn about tapirs, they'll soon discover cool things about them and how they are a special part of God's creation like every other animal.

This can happen with people too. When we meet someone new, someone who looks or acts different from us, we might think they're strange and that they won't fit in with our familiar friends. Sometimes we even avoid talking to them because we're afraid.

However, God tells us that we shouldn't be afraid and that we should treat everyone the same. He makes each one of us unique and He wants us to celebrate those things that make us special.

The next time you see a tapir:
Remember they may seem odd at first, but if everything and everyone looked the same, life would be boring. Celebrate the differences God gives us in all the people you meet!

Bible Verse

Romans 12: 4-5

Just as each of us has one body with many members, and these members do not all have the same function, so in Christ we who are many form one body, and each member belongs to all the others.

Mix'em & Match'em

To Do & Discover

In Thailand, there's a folktale that says tapirs were created out of the parts left over from the creation of other animals. Just for fun, let's pretend you need to write a story with an animal in it, but you can't use any animals you already know. You'll have to design your own. Let's see what happens!

What You Need:

Pictures of animals in books or magazines, or online

Paper for drawing, one piece for notes

Crayons or markers

What to Do:

1. Find pictures of at least five different animals.

2. Choose one thing from each animal to be a part of your new animal. Pick things like color, shape, size or part of the body. Make a list of what you choose on your notepaper so it's easier to remember.

3. Start drawing! When you're done, you can also draw in what it likes to eat and where it lives.

4. Name your animal using parts of the names of the animals you used. Don't write it on the front of the drawing though - keep it a secret for just a little while.

5. See if your family and friends can guess the name or tell you which animals inspired your new creature.

Extra Fact:

Unlike their parents, baby Malayan Tapirs don't have the white saddle. Instead, they are roundish, a light yellow-brown color and they have horizontal stripes along with some spots. Sound like anything else you've seen before? Maybe at the grocery store? They look a little like a watermelon with feet!

Toucan

What Do They Look Like?

If you see a bunch of different birds sitting in a tree, you'll have no trouble figuring out which one is the toucan - just look for a big, bright beak.

There are several different species of toucans, but they all have beaks that are large, brightly colored and slightly curved. Both males and females have this characteristic.

Also, while it might look like such a large beak would be heavy and make it difficult for toucans to move around, this isn't the case at all. Their beaks are made of thin bones and a substance that is similar to what your fingernails are made of. Also, the inside is like a honeycomb, which means there are hollow spots filled with air which also helps make them lightweight.

One well-known species is the keel-billed toucan. It's famous because its beak has four or five colors. It looks a kind of like a walking rainbow!

Where Do They Live?

Toucans live in the tropical jungles of Central and South America. In Belize, it is the national bird, just as the bald eagle is in the USA.

They live high up near the treetops in the part called the forest canopy. Toucans are also quite social and they live together in flocks. Even though their coloration actually makes good camouflage, it's not too hard to find them because they spend much of their time vocalizing and chatting with each other.

What Do They Eat?

Toucans are frugivores, which means they mainly eat fruit. Occasionally, they'll eat insects, or lizards too, but fruit is by far their favorite.

Their long beaks come in handy, giving them extra stretch to get fruit that is a little out of reach. The pointed end of their beaks also make good clippers allowing them to pick fruit a lot like you do.

More Interesting Stuff

Believe it or not, toucans rest curled up in a ball. First, they turn their heads so their beaks touch their back, then their tail bends toward the head tucking everything in underneath. Being able to do this allows them to nest in holes in tree trunks instead of building nests on branches like many other birds do.

A New View

In the Bible, there is a story about a man named Noah. One day, God told Noah to build an ark and gave him all the instructions he needed to get it done. Even though all his neighbors laughed at him, Noah did what God asked of him.

Once the ark was finished, Noah, his family, and a pair of each kind of animal on earth got on board. Then God caused rain and water to flood the whole earth. Nothing survived except the people and creatures that were on the ark.

After many months, the water dried up and Noah, his family and the animals returned to living on the land as they had before. Then God promised He would never destroy the earth with floods again. To remind everyone of that promise He provided a sign, a rainbow in the sky, just like the ones we still see today.

The next time you see a toucan:
Notice its curved multi-colored beak and how it reminds us of a rainbow. Take a moment to thank God for His promises to us.

Bible Verse

Genesis 9:14-15a

Whenever I bring clouds over the earth and the rainbow appears in the clouds, I will remember my covenant between me and you and all living creatures of every kind.

Everyday Rainbows

To Do & Discover

It's fun to look for rainbows after a rainstorm when the sun comes out, but did you know there are lots of other rainbows in our lives? Let's see how many rainbows you can find or create today.

What You Need:

You'll need to be able to remember the colors of the rainbow and what order they appear in. Use this memory trick: ROY G BIV which stands for red, orange, yellow, green, blue, indigo, violet.

Extra Fact:

When toucans are trying to attract each other, they toss food back and forth using their beaks, like you would play catch with a ball.

What to Do:

Start looking at life with "rainbow eyes", try to notice where you either see the colors of the rainbow together, or where you can put things together to make the right combination.

Here are some examples to get you started:

A) There is a candy that has the slogan "taste the rainbow." Hint: it starts with an S. If you eat them, remember the rainbow God sent to Noah.

B) Look in your closet. Can you organize it so that you see a rainbow of clothes? Is there a coat closet in your home? Try it there too.

C) Watch the sun coming through a glass, crystal, or maybe even a fish tank. Sometimes rainbows show up in unexpected places!

Wolverine

What Do They Look Like?

Some people have said that if you cross a weasel or a skunk with a bear, you'll know what a wolverine looks like. While that's not exactly accurate, they do have features that are similar to ones those animals have.

Wolverines have brown fur like a bear and a light stripe on each side, instead of on top like skunks. Adults grow to about three or four feet long and they only weigh twenty to forty pounds. Wolverines are in a family called mustelids, which does include skunks, along with otters and the mongoose.

Wolverines also have large feet, which makes it easy for them to walk on snow. This helps them catch prey in the winter.

Where Do They Live?

Wolverines like lots of room to roam. Adult males don't like to have other males around and each one can have a territory as large as 100 square miles.

They are only found in northern tundra, near the arctic circle on the continents of North America, Europe and Asia.

What Do They Eat?

Wolverines are both scavengers and hunters. They'll eat just about anything they can catch. Their main menu includes mammals like fox, rabbit, and small deer and birds. Besides eating what they can catch, they'll also eat carrion (animals that are already dead) if they can find it and occasionally plants and berries too.

In addition, since wolverines live in northern parts of the world where it is snowy and cold a lot of the year, they have a special adaptation to help them survive. They have a tooth that is super sharp and strong enough to tear through carrion even if it's frozen. That's one strong tooth!

More Interesting Stuff

Have you ever heard the phrase "small but mighty?" It definitely applies to wolverines. Even though they aren't much bigger than a medium sized dog, wolverines sometimes try to take away food from wolves and bears - and they win. They are considered one of the strongest animals on earth when you look at strength verses size.

A New View

Wolverines have been known to stand their ground and even fight animals that are much bigger than they are. In the Bible, there is a story of a person who fights a similar battle, not against an animal, but against a man who was considered a giant. That person was David.

David was a just a boy when he went to visit his brothers who were fighting in a war against the Philistine army. For over a month, a soldier called Goliath had been challenging King Saul's army to send someone to fight him one-on-one, but no one tried because he was such a huge man compared to them.

David told the king that he wanted to fight Goliath because that he knew God would provide whatever he needed to win. Saul believed this and let him go. He also tried to give David some armor, but it was too big. Instead, with strength from God, David was able to kill Goliath with just a stone in a slingshot.

The next time you see a wolverine: Remember that even though you are small, God can give you what you need to overcome anything.

Bible Verse

1 Samuel 17:45

David said to the Philistine, "You come against me with sword and spear and javelin, but I come against you in the name of the LORD Almighty, the God of the armies of Israel, whom you have defied.

Small But Mighty

To Do & Discover

Did you ever feel like you can't be strong because you're little or because you're a kid? Don't forget, wolverines are small compared to other animals, but they're also very powerful. Let's see if you're like a wolverine, small but mighty.

What You Need:

Your muscles

A variety of items from around your home

A basket or box

An adult to help you

What to Do:

1. Find a few things that are lightweight like a ball, a cup, a shoe. Picking them up is easy right?

2. Find a few heavier objects. Maybe cans of soup or vegetables, a box of pasta or a big thick book. Can you hold one in each hand? Can you stack two?

3. Now get your basket or box. Start placing items inside. How many can you hold? Make sure you stop before it gets too heavy. Can you figure out how much it all weighs? Did you know you could lift that much? See, you are small and mighty too!

4. Just as He does for animals, God gives us strength to use wisely. Remember to help your family and neighbors with those muscles of yours whenever you can. Do you know anyone who could use some help from your muscles right now?

Extra Fact:

Because wolverines are so shy and live so far apart, scientists aren't sure how many are left in the wild.

Wood Duck

What Do They Look Like?

In the Bible, there's a story about Joseph and his coat of many colors that his father had made for him. Well, God made a bird version of that coat- wood ducks are ducks of many colors! Males are brown, red, green, purple, white, black and yellow. Females aren't as fancy, but that's okay because duller coloration makes it easier for her to hide her ducklings under her wings.

Where Do They Live?

Wood ducks are common in the United States. They live in the Midwest, on both coasts, as well as in southern states. Those that live in northern areas migrate to the south, some as far as Mexico to avoid winter weather. They always live near water.

What Do They Eat?

Even though you may think that wood ducks eat a lot of fish because they live around the water, they actually like to eat seeds more than anything. Acorns are one of their favorites. They also like seeds from many aquatic plants, including one called duckweed.

Wood ducks eat some aquatic insects, too. In fact, babies don't eat seeds at first, only bugs they find in and near the water.

More Interesting Stuff

If you wanted to find a wood duck, you'd probably look at a pond or on a riverbank right? While they're often found on the water, believe it or not you can also find wood ducks high up in a tree!

Wood ducks like to make their nests in holes in the trunks of trees. This helps keep their young safe from predators. Sometimes the trees are close to the water, but sometimes they're deep in the woods.

In order to leave the nest, baby wood ducks have to do more than take their first steps - they have to take one big, huge, scary step! Mother duck leaves the nest first and flies down to the ground below. She then calls to her chicks to join her, even though they've never flown before and all their flying feathers aren't quite ready yet.

One by one, each chick jumps out and lands on the ground (sometimes they bounce a little, too). How far do they have to jump? The average nest height is thirty feet, which is as tall as a three story building, but sometimes nests are even higher! They definitely have to trust that Mom knows best.

A New View

Have you ever had someone tell you, "Just trust me"? Maybe they wanted you to try a new food like sushi, maybe they asked you to do something a little scary like swinging really high on the swings. How did you react? Did you believe what they said?

Have your parents or teachers ever told you to do something and just trust them? Maybe they told you how to solve a problem, maybe they said you should take your training wheels off your bike. Was it easy to do because you know they love and care about you?

God often asks us to trust Him, too. Sometimes He asks us to do things and we can't figure out what the outcome will be. That's when we have to take our leap of faith, just like the baby wood ducks, remembering our loving Father will not tell us to do something that will be bad for us.

The next time you see a wood duck:

Think about the giant jump that baby ducks take into the world. Remember they can do it by trusting their parent knows what's best, just like we can trust our heavenly Father God.

Bible Verse

Isaiah 12:2

Surely God is my salvation;
I will trust and not be afraid.
The LORD, the LORD, is my
strength and my song; he has
become my salvation."

Walk by Faith

To Do & Discover

When baby wood ducks are ready to leave the nest, they have no idea what the world is like. They are probably a little scared, but they take their big jump trusting they'll be okay. This activity will help you understand what it's like to trust when you don't know what's coming next.

What You Need:

A piece of cloth or a bandana to use as a blindfold

Someone to do this with you

What to Do:

1. Decide on a leader and a follower.

2. Have the follower go into another room while the leader sets up a short obstacle course. Make sure the follower doesn't have to do anything that could cause an injury.

3. Some things you might want to do: walk over a pillow, walk around a chair or table, bend down and pick up an unknown object.

4. Blindfold the follower so he/she can't see anything at all. The leader now takes the follower by the hand and leads him/her through the course. The follower needs to go through the course, trusting that the leader won't make them do anything harmful.

5. Switch places and try it again.

6. Think about whether you were nervous when you were the follower. Why or why not? What did you learn about trust?

Extra Fact:

Female wood ducks often return to the tree where they were born when it's time to have their own families.

Psalm 104

Vs. 1, 16-22, 24

[1] Praise the LORD, O my soul.
O LORD my God, you are very great;
you are clothed with splendor and majesty.

[16] The trees of the LORD are well watered,
the cedars of Lebanon that he planted.

[17] There the birds make their nests;
the stork has its home in the pine trees.

[18] The high mountains belong to the wild goats;
the crags are a refuge for the coneys. (rock badgers)

[19] The moon marks off the seasons,
and the sun knows when to go down.

[20] You bring darkness, it becomes night,
and all the beasts of the forest prowl.

[21] The lions roar for their prey
and seek their food from God.

[22] The sun rises, and they steal away;
they return and lie down in their dens.

[24] How many are your works, O LORD!
In wisdom you made them all;
the earth is full of your creatures.

CPSIA information can be obtained at www.ICGtesting.com
Printed in the USA
BVOW100007270213

313925BV00003B/3/P